Edmund Hatch Bennett

The Four Gospels from a Lawyer's Standpoint

Edmund Hatch Bennett

The Four Gospels from a Lawyer's Standpoint

ISBN/EAN: 9783337280970

Printed in Europe, USA, Canada, Australia, Japan

Cover: Foto ©Lupo / pixelio.de

More available books at **www.hansebooks.com**

THE FOUR GOSPELS

FROM A LAWYER'S STANDPOINT

BY

EDMUND H. BENNETT, LL. D.

BOSTON AND NEW YORK
HOUGHTON, MIFFLIN AND COMPANY
The Riverside Press, Cambridge
1899

NOTE

THE substance of the following pages was prepared by the author, largely as a matter of personal interest to himself. Finally he based a lecture or address upon the material which he had collected. This lecture he delivered many times, especially during the latter years of his life. As an introduction he sometimes used the prefatory matter which is now printed with the address. The author never himself prepared a copy for publication. Had he done so, possibly he might have revised its form somewhat. It is now printed substantially in the form in which he delivered it the last time.

BOSTON, October, 1899.

INTRODUCTION

CHRISTIAN friends from different churches and of many denominations, may I say a word or two, before commencing my address, on the subject of Christian unity? I say denominations intentionally, for I dislike to hear the words "sects" and "sectarians" applied to Christian brethren.

I am glad to have this opportunity to express my sympathy for, and my belief in, the plan of occasional union services in which we can all unite in one common service of praise and devotion. I doubt whether any more serious obstacle exists to the spread of Christianity, either at home or abroad, than the unhappy divisions and discords which have sometimes existed between different Christian bodies. It is time, in my opinion, to remember that here, as elsewhere, union is strength. The most successful army must have several divisions, — infantry, cavalry, and artillerymen ; but they are too world-wise to expect success by firing on each other, as they stand facing a common and united foe. So in the Christian army. There may be many cohorts, but there can be but one " captain of our salvation ; " and there should be but one banner over us, and that is the banner — the blood-stained banner — of the Cross.

Minor differences there may be and perhaps always will be in some points, especially in modes of worship and church organization, for there is no divinely appointed order of church worship. " There may be differences of administration, but it is the same Lord ; there may be diversities of operation, but it is the same God which worketh all in all." Some prefer a simple, others a more ornate form of public worship ; some assemble within plain, others within decorated walls. But whether the church windows be plain or colored, open both, and you look out upon the same world of sin, sorrow, and suffering, crying for our sympathy and aid. Whether the roof be plain or groined, raise up either and look aloft ; behold the same heavenly expanse of blue, with the same stars of hope beaming from its azure depths, or the same sun of righteousness arising with healing in his wings.

The choir may be a quartette, or vested, but from both the same songs of praise and devotion constantly ascend to the same Majesty on high. And these come from Christian authors of every name and every denomination.

You remember it was a Congregational minister who penned that devout hymn : —

> " I love thy Kingdom, Lord,
> The house of thine abode."

The Cary sisters of the Universalist fold have given us many devotional hymns, not the least popular of which is —

> " One sweetly solemn thought
> Comes to me o'er and o'er."

The Baptist author of " My country, 'tis of thee I sing," also wrote —

"The morning light is breaking,
The darkness disappears."

A Presbyterian taught us to —

"Stand up, stand up for Jesus,
Ye soldiers of the Cross."

While we are indebted to that sweet Methodist singer, Charles Wesley, for —

"Hark, the herald angels sing,"

" Soldiers of Christ, arise,"

" Jesus, lover of my soul,
Let me to thy bosom fly,"

and many, many others.

You know it was a Unitarian lady who breathed those saintly lines, sung in every church and every hamlet in the land : —

"Nearer, my God, to Thee, nearer to Thee."

Another member of the same communion, a layman, too, if I mistake not, declared that —

"In the cross of Christ I glory,
Towering o'er the wrecks of time ;
All the light of Gospel story
Gathers round its head sublime."

May I be permitted to remind you that Episcopal lips first uttered those touching words : —

> "Lead, Kindly Light, amid the encircling gloom,"
>
> " Abide with me ; fast falls the even tide,"

and —

> " Rock of ages, cleft for me,"

probably one of the most popular hymns in our language.

Nay, it is only just for us to acknowledge that a pious and devout Roman Catholic gave us that gem of devotional poetry : —

> " O Paradise, O Paradise,
> Who doth not crave for rest,"

and its twin sister, —

> " Jerusalem, the Golden,
> With milk and honey blest."

It was a Roman Catholic lady, who more than three hundred years ago, on her bended knees, in her solitary cell, poured forth the anguish of her soul in this piercing cry : —

> " O Domine Deus, speravi in Te,
> O care mi Jesu nunc libera me,
> Languendo, gemendo et genuflectendo
> Adoro imploro ut liberas me."

All which proves that the truth is — the simple truth is — that notwithstanding a difference in name and outward dress, the hearts of all true Christian men and Christian women beat in unison. Verily,

> " As in water face answereth to face
> So the heart of man to man."

However the external form of theological heads may differ, the shape of the human heart, the sound, healthy, human heart, is ever the same; and we are told that it is with the heart, and not with the head, that man believeth unto righteousness.

This unity of heart and feeling, I am glad to see, is manifesting itself now as never before in the many union services now being held throughout the land. In Lexington, Newton, Winchester, Boston, Bridgewater, Taunton, and many other places, such a movement has been attended with great success. The present attitude of Christian bodies towards each other is very different from that formerly prevailing. Such a meeting as this would have been impossible, I fear, fifty years ago. The omens are auspicious of even closer affiliation between Christians of different denominations. The Spirit of God is moving upon the face of the waters. Quench not the Spirit! The Gospel trumpet calls. Heed its summons! Some great transition is upon us. Yes, the morning light is breaking, the day is nigh at hand. I hope to see the time when the ministers of my own church shall be canonically permitted to open their pulpits to their brethren of other denominations. God speed the day!

CONTENTS

___

THE FOUR GOSPELS FROM A LAWYER'S STANDPOINT

IT is, as you know, a part of the lawyer's profession to examine and cross-examine witnesses, to detect their errors, and expose their falsehoods ; or, on the other hand, to reconcile their conflicting statements, and from seeming discord to evolve and make manifest the real truth. And this paper is the result of an effort, on my own part, to ascertain whether or not, independently of divine revelation, independently of the exercise of a devout Christian faith, independently of any appeal to our religious sentiments, the truth of the story told in the four Gospels could be satisfactorily established by a mere reasoning process, and by applying the same principles and the same tests to the Gospel narratives that we observe in determining the truth or falsity of any other documents, or any other historical accounts. While we claim no special favors in our investigations because of any alleged importance of the subject, it is only fair to expect that every one will come to this examination with an unbiased and unprejudiced mind, ready and willing to accept the same evidence of truth and honesty as in other inquiries.   Moreover, since we decide many important worldly matters upon the mere preponderance of evidence and arguments, why should we not adopt the same principles here?   It is not necessary in order to recommend the Gospel story for our adoption to insist that it be proved to a *mathematical demonstration*, and beyond the cavils of every doubter, or of every unreasonable skeptic.   Why not adopt that conclusion which has the higher degree of probability rather than the opposite?   If we choose neither, we practically reject both.   In secular matters, if seventy-five per cent. of everything that can be said on both sides of any subject leads to one result, we are generally ready to adopt that conclusion in preference to the other. It is, you know, not uncommon before deciding some important worldly matter to arrange the arguments *pro* and *con* in parallel columns, and thus be guided by their comparative weight to our final conclusion. Let us do so here.

I approach this subject, therefore, with a personal reminiscence. A few years ago, while writing an historical address for one of our Massachusetts cities, I came across, in a newspaper file of the Revolutionary period, a letter, or what purported to be a letter, written from that place, giving an account of a meeting held there, in 1774, and a copy of some patriotic resolutions passed thereat. The writer of that letter, if there ever was one, had long been dead; all the persons said to have taken part in that meeting were also gone; the printer and publisher who gave the account to the world had likewise vanished from the earth; there was no person living who could make oath or testify that such an occurrence ever actually took place. But yet I had no hesitation in adopting the account as genuine, and using it as an established event in the history of that town. The mere fact of the existence of such a document under such circumstances was *prima facie* proof of its genuineness and authenticity, quite sufficient to justify the acceptance of it as true until the contrary be proved.

What would have been my joy and confidence had I found four such letters, in four different papers, written by four different persons, giving an account of the same transaction? And although in a close comparison of these four accounts some variations should have been found as to the particulars of that event, would that overthrow all belief in the truthfulness of the accounts? Nay, would it not rather furnish stronger proof of their integrity? Had all four accounts been exactly alike, the suspicion would have been irresistible that one was copied from the other, or that all were taken from one and the same original. But substantial uniformity with circumstantial variety is one of the surest tests of truth in all historical narratives. The several accounts of many important battles of the world, and of many other historical events, vary in many particulars, and yet no one thereby has any doubt of their occurrence. The four portraits of the Father of his country, painted by four different artists, viz., Stuart, Peale, Sharpless, and Wright, though all taken about the same period of his life, vary so much in expression that you would scarcely know them to represent the same person, and yet the same George Washington undoubtedly sat for them all. The various editions of Gray's Elegy, and of some of Shakespeare's plays, differ as much as do some chapters of Matthew and Luke in their respective accounts of the same transaction. Indeed, what four of us could go away from this meeting, and give exactly the same account of what transpires here? What four witnesses under oath in a court of justice *ever* describe a transaction precisely alike? And yet their testimony is taken as reliable, in cases involving the most important interests, even of life and death. Indeed, judges and juries are apt to *discredit* a cause in which all the witnesses tell a long story in exactly the same words.

Let us apply the same principles to the subject matter of this address. The four Gospels exist; they purport to contain the history of our Lord Jesus Christ; the authors are not living; the characters they therein describe are no more. No man living knows *by direct personal knowledge* that these things were ever so. But why not apply the same rules of evidence and belief to scriptural narratives as to any other? Being in existence, and a minute account of passing events, they must be either genuine and true, or else a gross forgery. There is no alternative; for the self-delusion theory is preposterous. They were true when written, or were then an absolute falsehood. If the latter, they must *at that very time* have been known to be false, and an imposition on the credulity of those then living. These stories began to be published not long after the alleged crucifixion. Many persons were then living who could have easily refuted the statements of the evangelists had they been untrue. The enemies of Jesus were still alive and active. The Scribe and the Pharisee, the Priest and the Levite, still smarted under his repeated denunciations. They had the disposition, the opportunity, and the incentive to deny the story of the miraculous birth, the spotless life, the marvelous works, the sublime death, the astounding resurrection, and the glorious ascension of our Lord, had the then published description of these events been totally fabulous. But so far as we know, no person then living ever uttered a protest against these accounts, and for two thousand years they have been received and treated as veritable history.

Again, being written, they must have been written by some one. *There they are;* some persons wrote them ; and they must have been written by either bad men or good men; by liars or by truth-tellers, by forgers or by honest historians. That is a very elementary and simple proposition, but it is the key to the whole situation, one which I ask you to steadily carry with you throughout this investigation. Remember that every circumstance tending to *disprove* forgery tends on the other hand to prove truth; for they *must* be one or the other.

The question then is: Do wicked men write such books as these? Do liars proclaim that they *and all other liars* "shall have their part in the lake that burneth with fire and brimstone"? Does the thief denounce dishonesty, or the adulterer proclaim uncleanness, or Satan rebuke sin? If, then, these stories were not penned by wicked men, they must owe their origin to honest men; and if honest and truthful men wrote them, they must be honest and true narratives, and not a tissue of falsehoods. Is not the conclusion irresistible? Need we go farther? But let us look at the subject from four other standpoints.

I. PECULIARITIES OF EACH GOSPEL

ASIDE from the general considerations above alluded to, each Gospel itself contains internal and indirect, but cogent evidence of its own genuineness. I purposely omit all reference to the manifold external proofs of the authenticity of the Gospels, the number and force of which increase with every new discovery, and I confine myself wholly to inherent and intrinsic evidence thereof. Some of these illustrations I am about to give may be found elsewhere, and I lay no claim to originality, for nothing new or original can now be written on this subject. To present some old truths in a new setting is all I can reasonably expect to accomplish. Let us look at each Gospel separately, and see how its naturalness, its conformity to what we should expect, its harmony with the surroundings, tends to prove its truth.

St. Matthew.

Take first the Gospel of St. Matthew. He, and he alone, records the circumstance of Jesus paying tribute to the tax-collector of Capernaum (xvii. 24–27). How do we account for this? Why should Matthew be more likely to mention this particular fact than any other evangelist? When we remember that he was himself a tax-gatherer, and therefore especially interested in and observant of anything relating to his own profession, the answer is obvious. So again, Matthew informs us (xxvii. 66) that after Jesus's burial, the Jews went and "made the sepulchre sure, sealing the stone and setting a watch." How does it happen that Matthew alone mentions that fact? We must remember that the people of Judea, as has been justly remarked, were oppressively taxed under the Roman dominion, and that excessive taxation often leads to evasion, cunning, and fraud by the tax-payer; and to increased vigilance, caution, and close scrutiny on the part of the collector. Accustomed, therefore, to suspect fraud and evasion, Matthew would naturally be the most likely to notice and record a fact which tended to show that in so important event deception had been carefully guarded against. Would a man forging the four Gospels remember that he must make Matthew state these facts, and carefully make all the other historians omit them?

Naming the Apostles.

Again, in giving the names of the twelve apostles, a natural incident occurs which I regard as one of the strongest proofs of simplicity and truth in Matthew. The apostles are usually named in couples, thus: Simon and Andrew, James and John, etc.; one couple is described by both Mark and Luke as "Matthew and Thomas," Matthew's name being first in both stories; but

Matthew himself (x. 3), with the modesty of an honest and true man, says, "Thomas *and Matthew*," putting Thomas first and himself last. Is not this so natural as to be a sign of truth? But some skeptic may say, "This is only accidental; that don't prove much anyway." Read a little further and see. Matthew's occupation was then, as now, an unpopular and odious one, and the other evangelists therefore, when speaking of Matthew, make no reference to it; but Matthew himself, with true humility, says, "Matthew, *the publican*." Another instance of this same quality is found in the several accounts of Matthew's farewell feast to his former associates, when he forsook all and followed Jesus. Luke (v. 29) says, "Matthew made a *great feast* in his own house, and there was a *great company* of publicans and of others that sat down with them." Mark (ii. 15) agrees in this *complimentary description* of this event. But Matthew himself modestly omits all reference to himself and the magnitude of the feast, and simply says: "And it came to pass as Jesus sat at meat in the house," etc. (ix. 10), without even saying it was his own house; much less that he had invited a large company to his banquet. Is this forgery? If not, it is honest truth. Falsehood is pretentious, brazen-faced, crooked. Truth is modest, natural, artless. Straws, are they? Do not straws indicate the true course of the wind?

St. Mark.

Let us turn to St. Mark's Gospel. Here we constantly find explanation of Jewish terms and phrases which are not found in corresponding verses of Matthew about the same event. Thus in chapter vii. verse 2, Mark writes: "When they saw his disciples eat bread with defiled hands," they found fault; and then the writer adds this explanation, "for the Pharisees and all the Jews except they wash their hands oft, eat not." Again in verse 11, "If a man shall say to his father or mother, It is Corban,"

Mark adds, "that is to say, a gift." In chapter ii. verse 26, speaking of David eating the shewbread in the days of Abiathar, he explains again, "which is not lawful to eat but for the priests." In chapter v. verse 41, when he records that Jesus said to the maid, "Talitha cumi," he adds, "which is, being interpreted, 'Damsel, I say unto thee, arise.'" Again, Mark writes (vii. 34), "Ephphatha," and adds, "That is, be opened." Why is Mark so careful to explain all these Jewish terms and phrases when Matthew is not? If we remember that Matthew, himself a Jew, was writing for Jews, who understood such terms already, and Mark, himself a Gentile, was addressing Gentiles, who did not, we have the answer. What a skillful forger must he have been to have contrived all that!

St. Luke.

Luke also has many indirect proofs of naturalness. For instance, Luke traces the genealogy of Jesus upwards to Adam, as

the Gentiles did, because he was writing for
Gentiles, while Matthew, writing for Jews,
as we have said, reckons downwards from
Abraham, as the Jews always did. Still
more: In St. Luke's descriptions of miraculous cures, the natural and genuine char-
acter of his Gospel clearly appears. Thus,
while the others simply speak of Christ as
"healing *a* leper " and of curing a man who
had "*a* withered hand," Luke says the first
was "*full* of leprosy," and it was the *right*
hand of the last which was withered.

Again, the others say Peter's wife's mother lay "sick of *a* fever," but Luke writes
that she "was taken with a great fever." In
the account of the healing of the centurion's
servant, Matthew simply says the servant
"was sick of the palsy," but Luke with more
fullness records that " he was sick and *ready
to die.*" So in the healing of the daughter
of Jairus, Matthew merely states that her
father addressed our Saviour thus : " My
daughter is even now dead : but come and
lay thy hand upon her, and she shall live.

And Jesus took her by the hand, and the maid arose." But Luke, with more minuteness and tenderness of feeling, tells us that Jairus "fell down at Jesus' feet, and besought him that he would come into his house: for he had only one daughter, about twelve years of age, and she lay a dying. And Jesus took her by the hand, and called, saying, Maid, arise. And her spirit came again, and she arose straightway." And again, while three evangelists mention that Peter cut off the ear of Malchus, the servant of the high priest, they all stop there; but Luke alone, with his more acute observation, adds : "And Jesus touched his ear, and healed him." So also Luke alone mentions the compassion of the good Samaritan; he alone records the fact that the sleep of the disciples in the garden of Gethsemane was induced by extreme sorrow; that Jesus sweat great drops of blood, etc. Now why this more accurate observation and description by Luke of every circumstance of disease and of mental and physical suffering than can be found in any other historian of the same events ? What was there in Luke's history or life which qualified and induced him thus to note and describe all kinds of diseases so much more minutely than the others? Turn to Colossians (iv. 14), and you have the answer, where Paul, writing to the Colossians, closes his letter thus : " Luke, the beloved *physician*, and Demas greet you." Did the forger of Luke's Gospel conspire with the forger of Paul's Epistle, the one to put into Luke's mouth words which a physician would naturally utter, but without intimating that he *was* a physician, and the other to simply *call* him a physician, without giving any circumstances indicating it? Forgers do not rest content with such roundabout confirmations. On the other hand, truth-tellers do not trouble themselves to make their stories corroborate each other. But these are either forgeries or true tales. So much for Luke.

St. John's Gospel

also contains internal proof of honesty and genuineness. Thus in chapter vi. verse 66, soon after the miracle of the loaves and fishes, we read that "from that time many of his disciples went back and walked no more with him," and again in chapter vii. verse 5, that "neither did his brethren believe on him." What an admission for a writer to make if he were concocting a stupendous fraud to impose upon the community, viz., to openly proclaim to the world that the impostor, whose pretensions he was undertaking to bolster up, could not retain the confidence of those who were in daily personal contact with him! And this from a man who was not his *enemy*, but his first chosen disciple and his most devoted admirer! Candor might lead a *truthful* historian to make such an admission, but nothing would induce a fraudulent one to do so.

But still another striking characteristic

of genuineness is found in John's Gospel.
He omits all reference to many events
which the other evangelists record in full.
Thus, he makes no allusion to the tempta-
tion of Jesus by the Devil ; to the first
miraculous draft of fishes ; to the healing
of Peter's wife's mother, or the recovery
of the leper ; to the cure of the paralytic,
or of the withered hand, or of the two de-
moniacs ; to the parable of the sower; to
the stilling of the tempest, or the feast of
Levi to our Lord ; to the prophecy of the
destruction of the temple, or the parable of
the fig-tree ; to the transfiguration on the
mount, or to many other important events, to
some of which he was even an eye-witness.
Why is this notable omission by John of so
many scenes with which he was perfectly
familiar and which the other three evangelists record so fully ? If it be the fact that
John's Gospel was written long after the
other three had been published to the world,
as is generally believed, does not that naturally suggest that he probably thought it

unnecessary to repeat what they had already described so minutely ?

On the other hand, John alone mentions many interesting and touching incidents in our Saviour's life, about which all the others are entirely silent. Thus, he alone narrates the story cf John the Baptist at the time the Jews sent the Priests and Levites to interrogate him ; he alone describes the calling of Andrew and Simon, Philip and Nathaniel ; he alone records the marriage in Cana of Galilee ; the driving of the money-changers from the temple ; the visit of Nicodemus by night ; the meeting with the Samaritan woman at Jacob's well ; the healing of the nobleman's son ; the scene at the pool of Bethesda ; the parable of the good shepherd ; the restoring of sight to the blind in the pool of Siloam ; the raising of Lazarus, etc. In John alone do we read that sweetly tender address of Jesus to his disciples, which has since soothed many a sorrowing breast, " Let not your heart be troubled : . . . in my father's house are many mansions " (xiv. 1). Why does John record so many touching and tender events in our Lord's life of which others make no mention ? Do we not find the explanation in the fact that he was the disciple whom Jesus preëminently loved ; that he enjoyed in a special degree his Master's regard and confidence, resting his head so often on his Master's bosom ; that his mother was one of those who constantly followed Jesus and ministered unto him ; that of the four evangelists he alone was present at the transfiguration on the mount and at the agony in Gethsemane ; that he alone followed Jesus to the cross, and was present at so many other affecting scenes to which the rest were not admitted ?

Could we have more satisfactory evidence of probability and truthfulness than these several peculiarities in the four evangelists indicate ? What a consummate forger must he have been who could know and constantly remember all these particulars and never make a slip in his fabrications! The forger of the letters falsely attributed to Mary, Queen of Scots, or of the famous Parnellite letters some years ago, could not compare in ingenuity with a possible forger of the four evangelists. May we not believe, therefore, that each Gospel by its own internal peculiarities bears testimony to its truth and reality?

II. CONFIRMATIONS IN THE GOSPELS

B Y comparing the various Gospels with each other, we often find confirmations of their truth and veracity.

A notable instance exists in regard to *Herod's Servants.*

In Matthew (xiv. 1, 2) and Luke (ix. 9) we read that when Herod the tetrarch heard of the fame of Jesus, being perplexed thereat, he said unto his servants inquiringly, "This is John the Baptist; he is risen from the dead," "John have I beheaded, but who is this of whom I hear such things?" The inquiry at once arises, why did Herod address this question to his *servants?* What could *they* be supposed to know or care about Jesus, or about John the Baptist? Matthew gives no reason why, but on turn-

ing to Luke (viii. 3) we learn that one of
the followers of Jesus was Joanna, *the wife
of Herod's steward.* And in Acts (xiii. 1)
we are told that in the church at Antioch
there was a teacher named Manaen, "who
had been *brought up with Herod the tetrarch.*" No doubt, therefore, Herod supposed that the higher grade of his servants
could give him some information about
Jesus which he wanted to know, and it was
not strange, therefore, that he should address them as he did.

The Transfiguration on the Mount.

Again, after the transfiguration on the
mount, Luke says (ix. 36) that they who
had witnessed this remarkable event "kept
it close, and told no man in those days any
of those things which they had seen." But
he gives no reason for this extraordinary
silence on a subject so full of interest and
wonder, and which the witnesses thereto
would naturally be inclined to spread abroad.
But turn to Mark, and you will find the

explanation (ix. 9), where he records that as "they came down from the mountain Jesus *charged* them they should tell no man what things they had seen," etc. One narrates the command, but not the obedience; the other the obedience, but not the command. Is that a contrived variation, or is it the natural and accidental difference into which honest witnesses constantly fall?

The Passover.

Once more: When Mark tells us (vi. 31), that after the death of John the Baptist, Jesus said unto his disciples, "Come ye yourselves apart into a desert place and rest awhile," the writer adds, "for there were many coming and going," without giving any intimation of the reason why so many should be abroad at that particular time; but on turning to John (vi. 4) the missing link appears, for we learn that "the passover was nigh" at hand, and thus the cause of the traveling multitude is obvious, viz., they were all going up to Jerusalem to the feast.

The Samaritans' Disregard of Jesus.

Still again : In Luke (ix. 51, 53) we are told that Jesus on one of his journeys to Jerusalem sent messengers before him to a village of the Samaritans, to make ready for his coming ; but the Samaritans would not receive him, " because," to use the Scripture language, " *because his face* was as though he would *go to Jerusalem.*" Why should that be a reason for not receiving him ? What difference could it make to them whether he was going to *Jerusalem* or to some other city ? Luke does not tell us why, nor does he give us the slightest clue on the subject, but we learn it elsewhere. It is this : the Samaritans did not believe in Jerusalem as a place of worship : they had set up a temple in Gerizim in opposition to the holy city. As Jesus was known to be on his way to Jerusalem to worship there, it was only poor human nature that the Samaritans did not feel like paying him any particular attention when on such a journey.

The Denial by Peter.

In the denial by Peter a notable indirect confirmation or proof of veracity occurs. Thus, three of the evangelists say that when Peter was warming himself in the palace of the high priest, a maid saw him, and charged him with being a disciple of Jesus, but neither of the three intimate how she knew it to be so. How *should* a maid servant in the family of the high priest, the most exalted officer in the Jewish synagogue, know such a fact? Proud of her position in the first family in town, wearing the brightest and gayest dress of all her set, what should that dark-haired and dark-eyed Jewish maiden know or care about the lowly and despised Nazarene; much less as to who his deluded followers were? Turn to John (xviii. 17), and the mystery is solved. There we learn that the maid who thus addressed Peter was the very one who kept the door of the palace through which Peter had just entered. But how did that enable her to know that Peter was a *follower of Jesus?* Read John again (xviii. 15, 16), and we find that John first went into the palace with Jesus, leaving Peter standing outside, and then John came out, and as he was going out, " spake to her that kept the door, and brought in Peter," right past her. She saw John come in with Jesus, and then go out and bring in Peter, and remembering what he had said to her going out, she was not a very bright girl unless she could put this and that together, and guess pretty well what was going on. And this incident furnishes another corroboration of one evangelist by the others. John speaks of only one maid who thus addressed Peter. Others say there were two, while Luke says it was a man. But John himself further on indirectly confirms the other three because he says, in verse 25, that as Simon Peter stood and warmed himself, " *They* said therefore unto him, Art not thou one of his disciples ? "

Smiting of Jesus.

Again, in the last tragic scene of our Saviour's life, Matthew tells us (xxvi. 67, 68), that his murderers, after spitting in his face and smiting him with the palms of their hands, challenged him to say who smote him, as if that were an impossible question for him to answer. How could such a question be difficult? Could he not see who struck him, and in the face, too? Matthew gives no fact throwing light upon it, and none is there apparent. You could not understand it from Matthew alone. But turn to Luke, and the reason for such a question is obvious, for Luke says (xxii. 64), "When they had *blindfolded* him, they struck him on the face, and asked him, saying, Prophesy, who is it that smote thee?" Thus we see the force and significance of the question, addressed to a blindfolded man, which to another would have been too simple.

The Bearer of the Cross.

Matthew and Luke say that at the crucifixion of Jesus his cross was borne by one Simon, a Cyrenian, but they give no other particulars about him. Mark alone adds that Simon was the father of Alexander and Rufus. Why? Mark wrote his Gospel at Rome for Romans. But what had that to do with it? Turn to Romans xvi. 13, and we find that Rufus was a disciple of Jesus, and lived in Rome. How natural, therefore, that Mark, when writing to *Romans*, should specially refer to Rufus, who was then living among them, and whose father had been so closely connected with the awful tragedy of the crucifixion. And how natural that first the pity and then the love of Rufus should have been excited for Jesus by the fact that his father had borne the cross, and was an eye-witness to the awful sufferings thereon, the account of which no doubt he had often heard from his father's lips.

Division of the Garments.

One more instance of confirmation remains. The division of the garments of Jesus after the crucifixion furnishes a remarkable instance of the truth of the Gospel narrative as confirmed by other sources.

John informs us (xix. 23) that when the soldiers had crucified Jesus, they took his garments, "and made *four* parts, to *every soldier* a part." How is this? Why just four parts? Were there no more soldiers there, on such an extraordinary occasion as that? Yes, they had "the whole band" (Matthew xxvii. 27; Mark xv. 16). And a centurion's band is an hundred. Why were only four entitled to his garments? This is the explanation. Crucifixion as a mode of punishment was well known to many ancient nations. The common and familiar practice was to compel the person to bear his cross to the place of crucifixion, and to lay the cross upon the ground, one end slightly raised ; then the victim was laid upon it, with his arms and limbs extended, and four of the most brutal soldiers were selected to drive four large nails, or spikes, through the quivering flesh of his hands and feet, for which repulsive service they were entitled by custom to his clothes as a special perquisite. So John told the truth, — "four parts, to every soldier a part."

So much for confirmations by comparison.

III. VARIATIONS IN THE GOSPELS

SOME well-disposed persons, for the most part of the rather feeble-minded sort, are much troubled at the variations in the Gospel stories about the same event, and find many stumbling-blocks in their way.

Let us look at some of the events recorded in different words by the various evangelists, and we shall realize what is meant by the phrase "Harmony of the Gospels," and that mere variations are not . contradictions, but on the other hand often real confirmations of each other. Take, for example, the imprisonment of John, Baptist by Herod. Matthew tells us (xiv. 3, 4) that Herod had laid hold on John and put him in prison for the sake of Herodias, his brother Philip's wife, because John had told Herod that it was not lawful for him to have her, but Matthew nowhere intimates that they were *already married.* Mark alone (vi. 17) informs us that the marriage had actually taken place. Luke adds yet another reason for John's imprisonment, viz., because he had reproved Herod, not only for the Herodias matter, but also "for all the evils which Herod had done" (iii. 19). But there is no conflict or inconsistency in these different accounts; every word of every one may well be true.

Healing the Leper.

So in the healing of the leper, Matthew says (viii. 2), "Behold, there came a leper and worshipped him saying, Lord, if thou wilt, thou canst make me clean." Mark adds something different (i. 40): "And there came a leper to him, beseeching him, and *kneeling down* to him, and saying unto him, If thou wilt," etc. This additional fact of kneeling Matthew does not record. Luke (v. 12) mentions still another feature, viz., "The leper *fell on his face, and besought him, saying, Lord, if thou wilt,"*etc. These variations are only successive strokes on one and the same picture.

The Inscription on the Cross.

The inscription on the cross furnishes one more, and one of the best illustrations of unity in variety to be found in the New Testament. Mark (xv. 26) says it read, " The King of the Jews." Luke (xxiii. 38), " *This is* the King of the Jews." Matthew (xxvii. 37), " This is *Jesus* the King of the Jews." John (xix. 19), " Jesus of *Nazareth* the King of the Jews." Was there no cross on Calvary because of these variations, written as they were in Hebrew, Greek, and Latin (Luke xxiii. 38) ?

Is the story of Barabbas a myth, merely because one evangelist (John) says he was a robber, and two others (Mark and Luke). call him a murderer ? Was there no king of Tyre because in some places his name is spelled Hiram and in others Huram ?

Is there no true time of day, because all the clocks in your house strike at a different moment ?

These many variations lead to another suggestion. If these are forged tales, they were doubtless written by the same person, or by four different persons. How improbable that the same person should take the unnecessary trouble to make up four false stories about Jesus, in order to impose on the world, and at the same time make them so different from each other as to excite doubts in some honest and well-disposed minds, even to this day, as to the truth of any one of them !

On the other hand, how vastly more improbable that four different persons, at different times and in different places, should deliberately sit down without any apparent motive to write four similar fictitious stories without any knowledge of each other's work ; or, if they had such knowledge, that they did not make their stories agree better with each other ! It is too absurd to be worthy of even denying.

Here again we may learn from secular matters that the actual occurrence of some event is not to be doubted because of some discrepancy, or even some contradiction, in details between the different narrators thereof. For instance, some historians assert that Lord Stafford was condemned *to be hanged* for his alleged participation in the popish plot in 1680, while Burnett and other historians narrate that he was *beheaded*. But that he suffered death for the charge, though probably unjustly, no one doubts.

So in our own times there has been for more than a century a controversy as to the person who made the public proclamation of the Declaration of Independence, from the balcony of the old State House in Boston, on the morning of July 18, 1776. Many accounts assert that this proclamation was made by William Greenleaf, the high sheriff of Suffolk County; while as many more declare that it was by Colonel Thomas Crafts. But recent researches disclose the fact that Mr. Greenleaf, having a weak voice, first read the Declaration, sentence by sentence, to Colonel Crafts, who stood by his side, and then the latter, in his loud and sonorous tones, repeated the same to the assembled multitude below; and thus the seeming conflict is easily and naturally reconciled.

IV. INCONSISTENCIES IN THE GOSPELS

ET us now look at some of the alleged inconsistencies in the Gospel stories; in reconciling differences, let not the children of this world be wiser than the children of light.

The Healing of the Two Demoniacs.

Mark (v. 2) and Luke (viii. 27) say that *a man* with an unclean spirit coming out of the tombs besought Jesus to cure him. But does it follow that Matthew was false, because he says (viii. 28) *two men* met him? If there were two there certainly was one, and if there was one it does not prove that there were not two. But, as has been well said, there is an obvious reason why Mark and Luke mention only one. What is it?

There was only one who showed any gratitude for his deliverance, and his case therefore impressed itself the more on their minds since the duty of gratitude for blessings received was the special lesson they were seeking to inculcate.

And this expulsion of the devils and sending them into a herd of swine suggests another proof of reality and indirect confirmation. "There was," say the evangelists, "nigh to the city of Gadara, a herd of swine feeding." How could that be? The Jews were forbidden to eat swine's flesh. It was such an abomination to the Jews that one of them declared that he would die rather than eat it. How happened it that such animals were being raised about the city of Gadara, and great herds of them, too? Turn to Josephus, and we read that Gadara was a Grecian, not a Jewish city, and the Greeks had no aversion to swine's flesh.

The Alabaster Box of Ointment.

Again, because Matthew and Mark say that the woman with an alabaster box of ointment poured it *on the head* of Jesus, was John a falsifier when he says she anointed *his feet*, and wiped them with the hair of her head? Or because John mentions only Mary Magdalene as coming to the sepulchre on the morning of the resurrection, does it follow that the other evangelists are not to be believed because they state that other women accompanied her? Nay, John himself, although he gives the *name* of only one, indirectly confirms the others in their statement that more persons were present than Mary, for he says (xx. 2) that Mary, running to meet Peter, exclaimed, "They have taken away the Lord out of the sepulchre, and *we*," using the plural, "know not where they have laid him."

The Sermon on the Mount.

Another difference in the story about the
sermon on the mount seems to trouble some
minds wonderfully. Matthew (v. 1, 2, 3)
says, " And seeing the multitudes, he went
up into a mountain : and when he was *set*,
his disciples came unto him; and he
opened his mouth and taught them, saying,
Blessed are the poor in spirit," etc.

On the other hand, Luke says (vi. 17) he
"*stood* in the *plain*," — or "a level place,"
as the new version has it, — and lifted up
his eyes, and said : " Blessed be ye poor,"
etc. One says he was standing ; the other
that he was sitting. How is this? Remember this is the longest discourse Jesus
ever delivered, probably not wholly reported
either, and if he became tired of standing
before his sermon was finished, why
should he not sit down ? He was human
like the rest of us, except without sin. But
one says he went up the mountain; another that he stood on a level place. How

could that be? Did you never partly ascend a mountain and find a plateau, table-
land, or level place on its sides or between
its depths, where many people could easily
be assembled? Is not that exactly the way
it probably happened? Luke agrees with
Matthew (see vi. 12), that before he com-
menced his sermon Jesus went up into the
mountain to pray, and then he adds, in verse
17, that he came down and stood in a
level place, where he lifted up his eyes, and
said, "Blessed are the poor," etc. I do not
overlook the fact that tradition still points
out just such a " level place" between two
peaks called the " Horns of Hattîn," on the
road from Tiberias to Capernaum, as the
very spot where the sermon was delivered,
but I am suggesting that the combined
Gospel stories point to exactly the same
conclusion.

Miracle of the Loaves and Fishes.

Then came the miracle of the loaves and
fishes at Bethsaida. This miracle furnishes

a striking proof of the harmony and consistency of the Gospels, while using language apparently inconsistent. Thus Luke says (ix. 14) that the multitude sat down, in companies of about fifty each, whereas another asserts that they sat down "by hundreds." How so? This is another of the much vaunted inconsistencies of the Bible. How could these two expressions be true? Easily enough. If they sat one hundred in the front row and fifty rows deep, would there be any contradiction in the two statements? Would that not be a literal compliance with the words of Mark (vi. 40), viz.: "They sat down in ranks, by hundreds, *and* by fifties." How many would that be? Fifty times one hundred is five thousand; and therefore John, without saying anything of the manner of their arrangement or the order of their seats, simply says (vi. 10): "So the men sat down, in number about five thousand." Each writer uses different words, but all the statements harmonize and blend in one consistent whole.

But we are not quite through with this interesting story. One evangelist informs us that the next day after feeding the five thousand some of the people of Bethsaida, which, as you know, is *northeast* of the Sea of Galilee, took shipping and came over to Capernaum on the *west* side ; and when they found Jesus over there, they said, " Rabbi, when camest thou hither ? " (John vi. 25). Why did they put that particular question to Jesus ? Was it mere idle curiosity, or was there some special reason for their surprise and wonder at finding Jesus in Capernaum so early the next morning ? Let us see. Elsewhere we learn that in the latter part of the day of the miracle, the disciples took the *only boat* there was at Bethsaida to cross the lake to Capernaum, and Jesus was not with them, for he had gone apart into a mountain to pray. As there was *no other boat* left at Bethsaida, the people who thus addressed Jesus naturally wondered how he could have crossed that night so as to be in Capernaum early the next morning. Turn to Matthew and you will find how it happened (xiv. 25). He tells us that in the fourth watch of the night Jesus joined his disciples on their way over to Capernaum, "*walking upon the sea.*" And this was in the very darkest hours of the night ; the people in Bethsaida had no knowledge of Jesus's departure, and supposing he was still in the mountain on the east side behind Bethsaida, where his disciples had left him the night before, they might well be surprised at finding him so early the next morning over in Capernaum, on the west side of the sea, and therefore naturally exclaimed when they met him, "Why, Master, how in the world did you get over here this morning ? "

But still another interesting question arises : If the disciples had taken the *only* boat there was at Bethsaida on the evening of the miracle, how could the other people of Bethsaida, who addressed Jesus thus, have themselves gotten over to Capernaum the next morning ? Did some boats arrive at Bethsaida during the night? That was an awful night on Galilee. And in Matthew (xiv. 24) we learn that the disciples on their way from Bethsaida to Capernaum had a fearful time, "and their ship was tossed with the waves, for the wind was *contrary*." If the wind was contrary to the disciples, going westward from Bethsaida to Capernaum, it must have been favorable to other persons bound eastward *to* Bethsaida from the west side of the lake, and so it *might have* carried boats towards Bethsaida that night. But neither Matthew, Mark, nor Luke mentions any such circumstance. Turn now to John (vi. 23), where he says, "Howbeit there came other boats from Tiberias [which, like Capernaum, was on the west side of Galilee,] nigh unto the place where they did eat bread, after that the Lord had given thanks." And so a wind which to the disciples going southwest from Bethsaida to Capernaum would be "contrary," was exactly a wind to carry other ships that night from Tiberias north-eastward to Bethsaida ; and that is how these citizens of Bethsaida might have gotten over to Capernaum that morning.

What adroit forgers these evangelists were ; the one to narrate facts which would not easily have happened unless some boats had arrived at Bethsaida that night, but without saying so ; the other to have incidentally mentioned such arrival in his account of the transaction. I do not positively say that the people at Bethsaida did cross the lake by boat to Capernaum, for they might have gone by land around the end of the lake, as it is not over ten miles ; but I simply say that the facts stated in the several evangelists all harmonize with that view, although the story of no one alone brings it all out.

The Healing the Centurion's Servant.

Luke informs us (vii. 3) that when the centurion heard of Jesus, " he *sent unto him* the elders of the Jews, beseeching him that he would come and heal his servant." On the other hand, Matthew as positively declares that the centurion *went himself* unto Jesus, beseeching him (viii. 5). Some critics seem to think these two statements inconsistent. But are the two accounts so utterly irreconcilable? Let us see. Would it be impossible or unnatural that the centurion should *first send* the elders to Jesus, as Luke says he did, and after they had been gone for some time, becoming anxious and impatient at their long delay, that he should set out himself to plead in person with Jesus, — for this servant was "very dear unto him," — and so meet Jesus and the elders on their way back, as Matthew intimates he did. If this were all the discrepancy between the two accounts, it might be readily explained. But unfortunately, it is not, for Luke again, in verse 6, repeats the assertion that as Jesus was returning with the elders, the centurion *sent friends* to him, saying, "Lord, trouble not thyself," etc. But the Greek word used in this part of the story, and translated "sent,"

is ἔπεμψεν, not the same word translated
"sent" in verse 3, where he speaks of
sending the elders. That word is ἀπέ-
στειλεν, from ἀποστέλλω, which always means
to dispatch, to send off, etc. But this word
ἔπεμψεν, used in the 6th verse, means not
only to send, but also, according to approved
lexicons, "to lead, to escort, conduct, pro-
ceed with," and is used in that sense by
Homer and other writers. If Luke intended
to convey the same meaning in the second
place as in the first, why did he use a different word? Therefore the centurion might
himself be conducting or proceeding with
his friends, and so all meet Jesus returning
with the elders. Indeed, the language that
Luke puts into the centurion's mouth naturally imports that the latter was *personally
present* with his friends, as they met Jesus ;
for the centurion said, " Lord, trouble not
thyself, for *I* am not worthy that thou
shouldst enter under my roof. Wherefore
neither thought I myself *worthy* to come to
thee : but say the word only, and my ser-

vant shall be healed." Was not the man
who spake these words standing face to face
with Jesus? If so, it is true that the centurion *first sent* elders to Jesus, as Luke
narrates in verse 3 ; it is true that in the
second place he did go himself, as Matthew records ; it is true that when he went
himself, he was accompanied by his friends,
as Luke asserts in verse 6, and there is
now no contradiction, but all is in perfect
harmony.

The Case of Bartimeus.

As to the healing of Bartimeus, at Jericho,
a formidable discrepancy is thought to exist ;
viz., Matthew (xx. 29, 30) and Mark (x. 46)
speak of it as happening when Jesus was de-
parting from Jericho, while Luke (xviii. 35)
says, "It came to pass as he was *come
nigh unto* Jericho," etc. This is sometimes
thought to be a serious contradiction. Some
think it a *very* serious one, and their hearts
quake with misgivings. But look again. Is
this a variation, except in a comparatively

unimportant particular, a mere fringe of the
garment ?   Let us look at the miracle in the
perspective.   The important fact, the most
important fact is, did it take place at all, or
was it a mere invention ?   Three witnesses
declare it did, and no one says it did not.
All agree it was near Jericho.   All agree it
was in the presence of a great multitude ;
all agree that the party healed, be they one
or two, sat by the wayside begging.   All
agree in all the other essential particulars
of the miracle.   They differ in only one unimportant point.   Is the main story, then,
true or false ?   Did they all three fabricate
the tale, for you must convict all three of
false testimony to prove it untrue ?   Did
they copy from each other ?   Why, then,
did they not copy alike ?   If three witnesses
should testify in court to seeing a crime
committed, and all three gave the same
particulars, but two said it occurred in the
forenoon and one in the afternoon, or one
said it was on the north side of the road
and another on the south, would that invali-

date their testimony? The Bible stories, like other narratives, must be looked at in the perspective. If three witnesses in court agree in four particulars of the same transaction, and differ in only one, where is the preponderance of the testimony, — that they were all lying, or that one of them is mistaken? This and other differences in the Scriptures may militate against the doctrine of exact verbal inspiration; but that is not what we are endeavoring to maintain, but simply that the variance does not, from a legal standpoint, overthrow the positive testimony of the three evangelists that the event actually occurred.

The Two Thieves.

The different stories about the two thieves upon the cross furnish a very gratifying theme for criticism to some enemies of the Bible. You remember that two evangelists say that they who were crucified with Jesus reviled him, and cast the same in his teeth. But Luke tells us that one of them said, "This man hath done nothing amiss." Are those two accounts both false?

Would it be unnatural or impossible that both malefactors should have *at first* joined with the insulting crowd, and afterwards that the more tender-hearted of the two should have repented in the agony of approaching death, and exclaimed, " Lord, remember me when thou comest into thy kingdom " ?

Nay, in our modern criminal courts, how often does it happen that when two are arrested for some offense, they both deny it for a while to the officer, and yet afterwards one turns state's evidence, and convicts both of the offense.

How many a mother has called her two young children to her side for some disobedience of her command, and although both at first deny it, yet moved by her tender appeals the more conscientious of the two at last breaks down, and, choking with sobs, confesses the whole transaction.

Do not, therefore, I pray you, give up your Bible, your religion, or your God because of such flippant talk about the contradictions of the Gospels, come from whom it may!

Thus, by undesigned coincidences, by indirect confirmations, by unexpected corroborations, by natural and for the most part easily reconcilable differences, scattered throughout these four histories, may we be abundantly satisfied of the truth and harmony of the Gospels. The variations in these stories do not detract from their reliability, but rather the opposite. What would be our opinion of a man who denied the real existence of another merely because four photographs of him, one a front and one a back view, and two others of opposite sides of his face, did not present the same features? Is it not from the four views combined that you get the fullest and truest idea of the person portrayed? So from the combined pictures of the acts and doings of our Lord, in the four Gospels, or rather this fourfold Gospel, do we best comprehend the fullness of his life and power. What wonder, then, that Rousseau felt compelled to declare that if the Gospels were an invention, the inventor was greater than the hero, or a still later than Rousseau to assert that the forger of such a Jesus must have been superior to Jesus himself.

Conclusion.

This would be our conclusion if we were judging of the Gospel story simply by the light of intellect and of reason, and were endowed with no nobler and higher faculties; but there is a spiritual power within us, which makes the same answer; a faith which is higher than mere belief, as spirit is higher than mind, or mind higher than body. There is a part of us transcending the intellect, a part more deep, more boundless, and more sublime, than that of the mind; a part which "no fowl knoweth and which the vulture's eye hath not seen;" a part by which we may claim kinship with the cherubim and the seraphim; that part which enables us to see with the eye of a spiritual vision, and discern with a celestial insight; that faith which is "the substance of things hoped for, the evidence of things not seen;" which enables young men to "mount up with wings as eagles, to run and not be weary, to walk and not faint;" a faith which inspired the celebrated Congregational divine, Dr. Palmer, to pen that devout hymn, so full of trust, love, and confidence, —

> "My faith looks up to Thee,
> Thou Lamb of Calvary."

Let not, therefore, the criticism of the skeptic, the jeers of the scoffer, or the doubts of the agnostic disturb our calm confidence in the actual existence, the splendid example, and the divine attributes of him whose earthly life, miracles, and teachings are thus described in the four Gospels.

Nay, let us rather, with that abiding conviction derived from reason, faith, and love combined, confidently proclaim with the inspired apostle, "I know in whom I have believed;" or with that perfect and upright man of old, "*I know, I know,* that my Redeemer liveth." Yes, yes, —

> " Jesus lives, I know full well,
>   Naught from Him my heart can sever;
>   Life, nor death, nor powers of Hell,
>   Shall keep me from His side forever."

Amen.

www.ingramcontent.com/pod-product-compliance
Lightning Source LLC
Chambersburg PA
CBHW020241090426
42735CB00010B/1788